First Facts®

REALLY **SCARY** *STUFF*

SCARY
GHOSTS

by Jim Whiting

Consultant:
Elizabeth Tucker
Professor of English
Binghamton University
Binghamton, New York

CAPSTONE PRESS
a capstone imprint

First Facts is published by Capstone Press,
151 Good Counsel Drive, P.O. Box 669, Mankato, Minnesota 56002.
www.capstonepress.com

012011
006038VMI

 Books published by Capstone Press are manufactured with paper
containing at least 10 percent post-consumer waste.

Library of Congress Cataloging-in-Publication Data
Whiting, Jim, 1951–
    Scary ghosts / by Jim Whiting.
    p. cm. — (First Facts, really scary stuff)
    Includes bibliographical references and index.
    Summary: "Describes stories about ghosts and explores whether ghosts exist
or not" — Provided by publisher.
    ISBN 978-1-4296-3967-5 (library binding)
    1. Ghosts — Juvenile literature. I. Title. II. Series.
BF1461.W485 2010
133.1 — dc22   2009023387

Editorial Credits

Jennifer Besel, editor; Alison Thiele, designer; Marcie Spence, media researcher;
    Eric Manske, production specialist

Photo Credits

Archives Charmet/The Bridgeman Art Library International, cover; Capstone Press, 8; CORBIS/
Bettmann, 13 (left); Fortean Picture Library, 15, 16; Jude Huff-Felz and the Ghost Research
Society, 18; Library of Congress, 13 (right); Mary Evans Picture Library, 11, 12; Robert M. Place, 6;
Shutterstock/Morozova Tatyana (Manamana), 21; Shutterstock/PHOTOCREO Michal Bednarek, 5

**The legends and stories presented in this book may have different versions. The versions used
in this book are considered by researchers to be the most common telling of the event or story.**

TABLE OF CONTENTS

WHOA! WHAT WAS THAT?

In the glow of a campfire, your friends tell ghost stories. You jump when you hear creaks in the dark.

Do **spirits** of the dead really roam the earth? Some people think they do. Others don't believe in ghosts at all. Read on to learn about some scary tales. You decide if the ghosts are real.

spirit — the part of a person that is believed to control thoughts and feelings

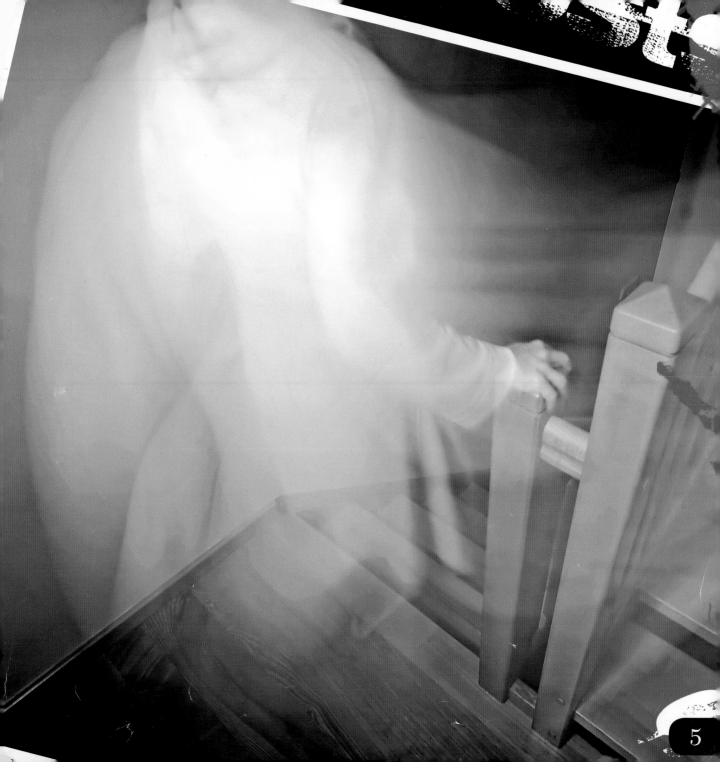

TERROR IN TENNESSEE

Strange things happened in 1817 on John Bell's farm in Tennessee. Family members felt something slap them. Then they heard an odd voice talking to them. The Bells believed the ghost of a witch was doing these things.

The Bells said the witch planned to kill John. In 1820, John got very sick and died. The family blamed the witch.

Did John Bell die at the hands of a witch?

The Bell family home

Many of the Bells' friends also said they heard the ghostly witch. But no scientific proof was ever found. Could a witch really have **haunted** the Bell farm?

haunt — to visit often, usually by ghosts

Did a Witch Haunt the Bell Family?

Yes General Andrew Jackson and other neighbors said they heard the witch too.

Yes People from all over the same county also claimed to have visits from the Bell witch.

Yes The people who later bought the Bell house said they heard odd noises in the house too.

No Poison was found in John's room. Someone else could have killed him.

No Most information about the haunting came from John's son Richard. But Richard didn't write about it until many years later. He could have made it up.

No Richard was 6 years old when he says the events began. He may have been too young to know what was going on.

THE GHOST SHIP

The story of the ghost ship *Lady Lovibond* began on Friday the 13th, 1748. The ship's captain had just married. But the ship's **mate** was in love with the captain's new wife. According to legend, the angry mate crashed the ship. Everyone onboard drowned.

Years later, sailors claimed to see the ship on the **anniversary** of the crash. Could the ghostly *Lady Lovibond* still sail the seas?

mate — a ship's officer

anniversary — a date that is remembered because something important happened

MR. PRESIDENT?

One night in 1865, Abraham Lincoln left the White House to see a play. That night, the president was shot. He never returned home. Or did he? Since the 1920s, people have claimed to see and hear Lincoln's ghost in the White House.

Look closely. Some people think Lincoln's ghost floats behind his wife, Mary. What do you think?

Queen Wilhelmina was staying in the Lincoln Bedroom when she claimed to see the ghost.

Queen Wilhelmina

One famous story was told by Queen Wilhelmina of the Netherlands. While staying in the White House, the queen heard knocking. She opened the door. The queen said she saw Lincoln's ghost standing right in front of her!

BAD DOG

A horrible ghost **hound** called Black Shuck is said to haunt England. People say this beast is as big as a calf, yet leaves no footprints. Its eyes glow red. Chains rattle around its neck. Some say anyone who sees Black Shuck will die in a year.

hound — a hunting dog

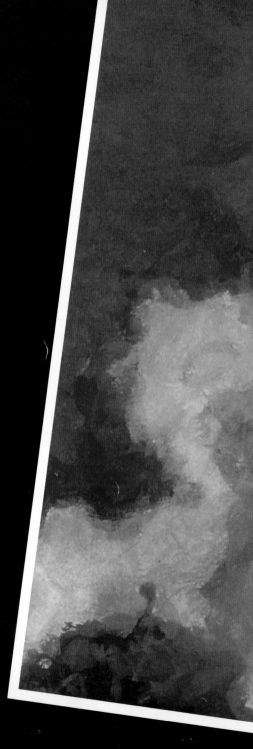

GHOSTLY GRAVEYARD

Bachelor's Grove Cemetery is in Chicago, Illinois. People say this cemetery is one of the most haunted places in the world. A floating house is said to appear out of nowhere. The mysterious White Lady wanders under the full moon. Stories of a two-headed ghost have frightened many people.

A strange blue light glows in Bachelor's Grove Cemetery. Could it be a ghost?

Researchers took pictures at Bachelor's Grove to try to see ghosts. Pictures taken there show odd lights and cloudy shapes. Could some of the shapes be ghosts?

Some people believe this picture shows a ghost in Bachelor's Grove Cemetery.

Is Bachelor's Grove Cemetery Haunted?

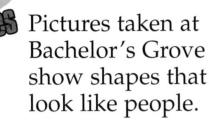

Yes Pictures taken at Bachelor's Grove show shapes that look like people.

Yes Many researchers think ghosts cause cold air. Researchers have found cold spots in Bachelor's Grove. The temperature in some spots feels colder than the places around it.

Yes More than 100 ghost sightings have been reported at Bachelor's Grove Cemetery.

No Problems with the camera or film could have caused the shapes in the pictures.

No Some historians believe the reports were made up to draw people to the cemetery for tours.

No Many people visit the cemetery and never see, hear, or feel a ghost.

THE HAUNTED TOWER

The Tower of London was used as a prison for many years. Prisoners were **executed** in the tower. Stories say the ghosts of people killed there still haunt the tower.

Ghost stories like the Tower of London might send shivers down your spine. But are the stories true? Or are ghost stories just made up for a good scare? No one knows . . . yet.

execute — to kill someone as punishment for a crime

Tower of London

GLOSSARY

anniversary (an-uh-VUR-suh-ree) — a date that is remembered because something important happened on that day

execute (EK-suh-kyoot) — to kill someone as punishment for a crime

haunt (HAWNT) — to visit often, usually by ghosts

hound (HOUND) — a hunting dog

mate (MATE) — a ship's officer

spirit (SPIHR-it) — the part of a person that is believed to control thoughts and feelings; the spirit is sometimes called the soul.

READ MORE

Hile, Kevin. *Ghost Ships.* Mysterious Encounters. Detroit: KidHaven Press, 2009.

Krensky, Stephen. *Ghosts.* Monster Chronicles. Minneapolis: Lerner, 2008.

McCormick, Lisa Wade. *Ghosts: The Unsolved Mystery.* Mysteries of Science. Mankato, Minn.: Capstone Press, 2009.

INTERNET SITES

FactHound offers a safe, fun way to find Internet sites related to this book. All of the sites on FactHound have been researched by our staff.

Here's all you do:

Visit *www.facthound.com*

FactHound will fetch the best sites for you!

INDEX